Preaching Theology

By

ERIC BAKER, M.A., Ph.D.

LONDON : THE EPWORTH PRESS

THE EPWORTH PRESS
(FRANK H. CUMBERS)
25-35 City Road, London, E.C.1

NEW YORK   TORONTO
MELBOURNE   CAPE TOWN

RUSH & WARWICK (BEDFORD) LTD., HARPUR PRINTING WORKS, BEDFORD.

Contents

PREFACE

A word of explanation seems necessary to meet the obvious criticism that this book is a superficial treatment of great themes. The chapters it contains originally appeared as articles in *The Preachers' and Class Leaders' Magazine* and are now collected and published in response to requests that they might be available in book form. Readers are asked to bear in mind that the only intention of the articles was to suggest some useful lines of approach which preachers might themselves develop in their own way.

Eric Baker

1

By Way of Introduction

THIS book is about theological preaching, and before considering any particular Christian doctrine it would be well for us to deal with a prior question and see the vital importance of this type of preaching. Many preachers would doubt its wisdom and efficacy, just as many professing Christians would disavow any concern with Christian doctrine and even suggest that their discipleship is genuine and effective because it is expressed in action, and not mixed up with theology.

This is, however, a profound mistake. In no other field would men countenance such a nonsensical and disastrous divorce of theory from practice. Doctrine is not an obscure subject to be studied by a few specialists who have nothing better to do. On the contrary, it is that by which we live. Theology stands to discipleship in the same relationship as a knowledge of botany to the planting and tending of a garden. A sound understanding of the first is an indispensable condition of a satisfactory achievement of the second. Christian behaviour springs from Christian belief. No current opinion is more beside the mark than that which stresses the primacy of action. It is belief that is primary. Action is always secondary. As a man believes, so does he both behave and become. Actions are a kind of barometer revealing the true state of a man's faith. As the weather is more fundamental and important than the barometer so is a man's belief more fundamental and important than the actions which reveal it.

There was an occasion when our Lord's disciples asked Him, 'What must we do that we may work the works of God?' Swift and sure came the reply: 'This is the work of God that ye believe.'

A little reflection will show that the troubles and distresses that afflict us have their origin in unbelief. Mankind may be split into many different divisions by age, race, language, wealth, sex, etc., but no cleavage is so deep and significant as that between belief and unbelief.

The world in which we live is largely a world of unbelievers. Ancient beliefs, which have for centuries been accepted as axiomatic, are today called into question. ' Is there a God? ' ' What is He like? ' ' What is man? ' ' Has he an eternal destiny? ' Such ultimate questions would receive no generally accepted answer today. The confusion thus existing in men's minds produces corresponding chaos in the realm of morals. This is only to be expected. Suppose doubt were suddenly cast on the long accepted view that two and two make four, what indescribable confusion would speedily ensue in almost every department of life; but that is precisely the kind of thing that has happened in the spiritual realm. Man has turned from God. In consequence he has become unsure of himself, and all confidence and stability has departed from the lives of men and nations.

Against such a background what shall we preach? Can we hope to lead men out of darkness into light, out of chaos into order, out of strife into peace by general exhortations? Surely not. Our only hope is to restore man's faith in the ultimate realities, in God, in man's nature and destiny, in the validity of spiritual values.

The truth we proclaim is truth embodied in a tale. Our message is based on certain happenings in history 1,900 years ago, but we cannot rest content by a mere recital of the facts. The story becomes good news when we interpret the facts and proclaim it to be a story about God. It is something God did once and for all. It is the revelation in time of God's character and eternal purpose. That is why it is worth proclaiming. From it we gain our understanding, not only of who God is and ever will be, but of what man is in God's plan and can become by God's grace. On that has grown up the whole

system of Christian ethics, which, directly or indirectly, has
produced all that is gracious and worth preserving in Western
civilization.

But this is theology. It is ' the faith once for all delivered
to the saints ' for which we are bidden to ' contend earnestly '
It has been committed to us as a heritage to pass on. Let us,
therefore, consider it together afresh.

2

The Doctrine of God

' PREACH about God,' a certain bishop is alleged to have
enjoined a young minister seeking advice, ' and preach about
twenty minutes.' The second rule is a good one, but the
first should be unbreakable. If it be true that nothing matters
so much about a man as what he believes, we can go on and
say that what matters most in his belief is what he believes
about God. This will determine what he believes about himself, about other people and ultimately about everything else
in life. The Gospel is good news about God. Let us,
therefore, preach about God.

As Christian preachers, our proclamation of God will be
based on our conviction that God's character and purpose
have been once for all revealed in Jesus Christ. Christians
are not alone in believing in God. Jews, Mohammedans,
and many others do the same. What makes Christianity
Christianity, and not some other religion, is the belief that
God, the Creator of the world and everything that is in it,
became Man for us and our salvation.

This central Christian conviction governs all our thought
about God and should similarly govern our preaching.

Whatever aspect of Christian truth we may be dealing with
in a particular sermon, there should be in our own minds,
and, before we are finished, in the minds of our hearers, a

direct connexion between what we are saying and the central
Christian truth of the Incarnation. This does not mean that
all our sermons should be on the same theme. Heaven forbid !
In the last sermon I was privileged to hear, the name of Jesus
was never mentioned. That was a defect, and of many sermons it would be a final condemnation. On this occasion,
however, the sermon was redeemed by the fact that not only
did the whole utterance breathe the Christian spirit; it also
contained scarcely a sentence which could have been framed
without our Lord consciously in mind. In that it resembled
I Corinthians, chapter thirteen. The whole field of life and
thought is open to us, but it does mean that just as the
churches in which we preach only exist at all because of that
truth, so our message should be a message which in some form
proclaims and applies that truth. Let us see how this principle works out in one or two particular ways : We shall
often want to speak of God's glory in creation. With others
outside the Christian tradition, we acclaim Him Maker of all
things visible and invisible and we sense His presence in the
majesty and beauty of the created world. For Christians,
however, there is always a difference. I recall a talk I had
with a Church member during my ministry at Harrow on the
familiar theme of worshipping God in nature. My friend
asserted most vehemently : ' I assure you the presence of
Jesus is more real to me if I stand on Harrow Hill and gaze
over the landscape than if I sit in a pew in our church.' Un-
wittingly she had betrayed herself. She was pleading for a
sense of God's presence in nature, but because she had been
cradled in the Christian tradition, it was Jesus of whom she
spoke. Thereby she made it clear that she invested the
character of the God, whose presence she claimed, with those
qualities which no contemplation of the beauty of nature
would have revealed to her, but only God Himself in that
revelation in Jesus Christ, which led to the foundation of the
Church, and which is preserved for us by the Church's witness
and worship.

So always when we preach about God's majesty and power we shall do so as those who have in Jesus Christ the key to an understanding of His character and purpose. A good sermon could be made by bringing together in contrast the opening words of Psalm 19 : 'The Heavens declare the glory of God and the firmament sheweth His Handiwork,' and John 1^{14} : 'The Word became flesh and dwelt among us and we beheld His glory.' Nature can reveal God's majesty and power; only Jesus Christ His character and purpose.

Similarly when we take one of the many themes which deal with God's immediate influence on our minds and hearts. The Christian preacher has one overwhelming advantage when he seeks to awaken men to God's reality and presence. God Himself is his ally. Otherwise his task would be hopeless. God Himself has been addressing every member of our congregations every day of their lives. All the preacher need do, indeed, all he can do by his words, is to help men to recognize God's touch upon their lives.

This is what separates man from the rest of creation. God made mountains, but He doesn't address them. God made the beasts of the field, but He doesn't address them. God made men and addresses them continually. Not only so, but men and women are capable of responding to Him.

Once again the revelation in Jesus Christ is the determinative factor. As through Him we know the character and power of the God who is the Creator of the Universe, so through Him we know also the character of the God who speaks to us in the intimacy of our souls. He is the same God, for God is One. He was before all time, is now and ever shall be, and He has been revealed once and for all in Jesus. His is the Kingdom, the Power and the Glory for ever and ever. It is He with whom we and all men have to deal. On the issue of that supreme encounter hangs our eternal destiny.

3

The Omnipotence of God

ONE of the first things most of us were taught about God i
that He is almighty. To Him alone belongs all power. Suc
a belief leads to awkward questions which need to be face
if we are to commend our message to men. What do w
really mean when we ascribe omnipotence to God? If Go
can do all things, what in fact is He doing at the moment?

Let us consider how the idea arose. The word 'Almighty
is scarcely a New Testament word. It does not occur at al
in the Gospels and appears only once in the writings of Paul
though it is used several times in the Book of the Revelation
When it does occur it always means 'Lord of Hosts'. Bu
what are the 'hosts'? For an answer we may turn to a
passage in Isaiah 'Lift up your eyes on high, and see wh
hath created these, that bringeth out their host by number :
He calleth them all by name' (Isaiah 40²⁶). The 'Lord o
Hosts' is the being who rules over all nature. He is Lord o
all places and things, including men and women. This conception was especially important to the early Christians a
soon as the faith burst the narrow confines of Judaism and
was preached to the inhabitants of the countries around the
Mediterranean basin.

These first Christian missionaries were intent on asserting
the freedom of men from the malign influence of fate and of
the countless evil spirits with which the demon-ridden
paganism of that day believed the world to be infested. In
contrast to this, the Christians, like the Hebrews, believed in
one God Almighty who was in control of and superior to all
the powers in the universe. This was of course eminently
sound teaching, but with the passing years that original meaning was gradually modified until, in its English form,

Almighty' came to be used in the sense of being able to do anything. Men came to attribute to God power like our own, only on an unlimited scale. We are powerful within limits. God is all-powerful and can do anything.

It need scarcely be said that this is a sheer caricature of the original and has led to much unsound thinking. Once it is agreed that God can do anything, it is dangerously easy to make that the ground for believing that He has actually done all sorts of absurd things. To be capable of anything is hardly a complimentary description of anybody. It cannot be too strongly emphasized that this kind of reasoning is radically false.

Let us begin again with the original belief. To the early Christians as to the Jews, the idea of natural law, so familiar to us, was entirely unknown. So far from believing in the uniformity of nature, they thought that anything might happen anyhow, and if some extraordinary event did occur, they explained it as due to the capricious activity of some power who might or might not be good. Christian teaching transformed this belief by preaching that the one God, the Creator and Sustainer of the universe, is good and that therefore men are not at the mercy of capricious spirits.

It was a later and erroneous development of this doctrine that tended to see God's activity—not in the uniformity of nature, but outside these natural processes. One ludicrous form of this is still to be found in the terms of many insurance policies where certain types of unforeseen calamity are excluded from the provisions of the policy as being 'Acts of God'. The legitimate but quite wrong inference might be drawn that God is not at work in the ordinary processes of life and death, but is rather a Divine conjuror, a tremendous abstraction of power, possessed (as I read somewhere but can't remember where) of infinite velocity but no direction.

Happily the Christian believer is not committed to any such ridiculous doctrine of Divine omnipotence.

If then omnipotence does not mean limitless and unconditioned power, what does it mean? To what are we committing ourselves when we describe God as 'Almighty'?

I would suggest that 'power' is an idea that can only be understood in the light of the character of him who possesses it, and the purpose he seeks to achieve. If this be so, the omnipotence of God can only be understood as we interpret it in the light of God's character and purpose. These two together determine the meaning of the idea of 'power' as applied to God. A consideration of these two factors will help us to grasp the meaning of this otherwise unintelligible doctrine.

First of all, then, in the exercise of His power God is bound by His own character. He cannot deny Himself. God is good. To believe that is much more important than to believe that He is able to do all things. It is inconceivable that God should ever do, or wish to do, anything inconsistent with His own character of goodness. It is in relation to God's own goodness that for the believer the categories of good and evil have any meaning. That which is in harmony with God's character and will is good, that which is contrary to the same is evil. God, therefore, cannot make true what is false. He cannot make it a blessed thing to be wicked. God cannot do wrong. His inability to do so resides in His character.

Secondly, God's power must be defined in relation to His purpose. This is true of all power. Power in itself is significant only when it is related to some object in view. In terms of brute force an elephant is more powerful than a woman, and, if ability to forge a way through a virgin forest is what is required, the comparison still holds good; but, if something entirely different is desired, such as threading a needle, an elephant is futile and impotent. It is when we come to consider power in relation to the end in view that we begin to see our way through the difficulty, with which the unbeliever is so fond of confronting us, of reconciling our belief in a God who is at once wholly good and almighty with the present state of affairs. A perfect Creator, we are told, who is also all-powerful, should have been able to make a perfect world without the existence of evil and all the dreadful consequences for men and for society which evil brings in its train. But such a dilemma rests on the assumption, for which there is no foundation, that such a Creator would desire above everything else to make all his creatures immediate possessors of unalloyed happiness. As quite obviously He has not done that, the conclusion to be drawn is that God is either not entirely good or not all-powerful.

But what if such reasoning is based on a complete misconception of God's purpose? What if God has some nobler purpose in mind? Such is indeed the Christian view. We believe that God created men and women with a view to their displaying a quality of character which is only possible if they are free to choose it and, therefore, free also not to choose it. A world in which men are happy but not free is not necessarily a better world than one where men are endowed with the privilege and responsibility of freedom, which, if used in the right way, enables them to respond to God's call and co-operate with Him in the adventurous achievement of His sovereign purpose for them. Almost all men cherish freedom above all things and one effective way of meeting the unbeliever who confronts us with the dilemma we are considering is to throw the challenge back to him and ask him whether he would be willing to pay the price, which would be loss of moral freedom, if he could thereby make this world the kind of world he so light-heartedly assumes would be the best of all possible worlds.

The Christian view is that, by endowing men with at any rate a measure of delegated freedom, God reveals His power. If He could only keep His children in cotton wool, as it were, He would be weaker and less perfect than we know Him to be. He has given us freedom and He will never retract the gift, for to do so would be a confession of defeat involving the final frustration of His holy purpose. God is good and His weapon is love. When we say we believe in His omnipotence, we are confessing our faith in the omnipotence of Holy love.

Finally, let us see how God's revelation of Himself in Jesus Christ vindicates this outlook at every point. We speak of Him as ' Christ, the Power of God ' (1 Corinthians 1^{24}), but as men often assess power, He was weak. He had no wealth, no position, no power to command. Nor is His story that of one who began without these things and acquired them. Beginning with a manger for His cradle, He ended with thorns for His crown and a cross for His throne. But in Him God's goodness and God's love found perfect expression. The powerful things in the world overcame Him. Jewish religion and Rome's imperial power overwhelmed Him. But did they? Where are they now? The one is not a world force, the other is only in the history books. Kings cast their crowns before the Cross. The Holy Love of God, apparently defeated on Calvary, has been winning ever since, and after nineteen hundred years the Cross, the symbol of man's cruelty and sin, bears His message and is the ' power of God unto salvation unto everyone that believeth '.

We live in a world where new and dreadfully powerful forces are within man's grasp. The very existence of such power and the possibility of its misuse is enough to strike fear into the bravest heart. But the only power that can bring abiding blessing to men is the power of holy love. We believe in God the Father Almighty, in the omnipotence of Holy Love, in ' Christ the power of God '. Our calling as preachers is to proclaim that faith and as disciples to act on it.

The Omnipresence of God

I HEARD some years ago of a little girl in Edinburgh who was overheard saying her prayers on the evening before she was coming south for a holiday. After her customary prayers she added words to this effect: 'And now, God, I shall not be able to talk to you again for a while, as I'm going to England tomorrow for three weeks; but I will get into touch with you immediately on my return.' Although she did not realize it, that little girl was revealing a well-known characteristic of primitive religion. There is more than one parallel to that story in the Bible.

When Jerusalem was sacked and the Hebrews were carried away into captivity, it is recorded that one evening after the day's work was done, some of their Babylonian captors addressed them as they sat by the river bank: 'Sing us one of the songs of Zion' (Psalm 137³). 'How shall we sing the Lord's song in a strange land?' came the reply. Their religion was so bound up with the holy city, the heir to all God's promises, that they could not believe that their God could be a comfort and a hope to them now they were in exile far from home. Or again, we recall how when on occasions the Ark of God was captured, the first thing to be done was to regain possession of it. The Ark of God symbolized God's presence and it was difficult for the Israelites to realize that presence if the Ark was in enemy hands. That such a primitive conception was not peculiar to the Hebrews is illustrated by the naïve excuses with which the servants of the King of Syria sought to console their royal master after his army suffered an unexpected reverse at the hands of the Israelites: 'Their god is a god of the hills' they explained, 'therefore they were stronger than we: but let us fight against them in the plain, and surely we shall be stronger than they' (1 Kings 20²³).

In a geographical sense it would doubtless be true to say that this conception has been outgrown today. The prayer of the little Edinburgh girl is regarded as an attractive piece of childishness and no more. Such an idea belonged to the childhood of the race. If God is not everywhere, He is not anywhere. People either believe in God or, more often, they do not believe in Him; but nobody believes in a God who is in some places but not in others. Even in Old Testament times a worthier view was beginning to prevail. 'Whither shall I go from thy spirit?' asked the Psalmist, 'or whither shall I flee from thy presence? If I ascend up into heaven, thou art there : if I make my bed in Sheol, behold, thou art there : if I take the wings of the morning, and dwell in the uttermost parts of the sea; even there shall thy hand lead me, and thy right hand shall hold me' (Psalm 139[7-10]). It was the Psalmist's deep religious insight which led him to this conviction rather than the philosophical impossibilty of any other view.

This dawning consciousness of God's omnipresence came to its fulfilment in the New Testament. It is implied in all our Lord taught about God. Such a God as Jesus revealed could only be omnipresent. He is eternal and as independent of space as He is of time. As we have seen, there was nothing remarkable about such teaching in a Jewish environment, but when the message of the Gospel was carried by the apostles beyond the narrow confines of Judaea and Galilee into the wider world of Asia Minor and Eastern Europe, it came as a liberating influence to peoples who still believed in the existence of a myriad demonic powers of various kinds and degrees, who needed to be appeased. To such men the proclamation that God was One, and not ten thousand times ten thousand, and that His name was Love, was indeed a word of hope and power.

Do those who listen to us need this word today? There is a sense in which they do not. We are none of us likely to have in our congregations folk who believe that the God we worship exercises His sway within certain geographical limits. But is the same thing true in the realm of experience? The drama of Job opens with a scene in the courts of heaven when the sons of God come to present themselves before the Lord, and Satan came also among them. The Lord is recorded as asking Satan with pardonable pride. 'Hast thou considered my servant Job? For there is none like him in the earth, a perfect and an upright man, one that feareth God and escheweth evil.' We remember how Satan made reply. ' Job's religion' he said, in effect, 'is tainted with corruption. It is a fairweather religion. He has been the object of your special protection. Withdraw that protection. Let Job and his family be subject to the chances and changes of human experience like everybody else, and see then what this much-vaunted piety of his is worth.'

Here is a test of faith with which every man is faced on occasions. There come times when all of us are tempted to say : ' Where is God in this that is happening to me?' Is God omnipresent in that sense? It is safe to assume that in every congregation of any size there will be some who are feeling like that. What is the word we have to speak to them?

There is no question what answer Paul would give. ' To them that love God all things work together for good ' (Romans 8²⁸). The whole of the celebrated eighth chapter of Romans, from which that text is taken, constitutes Paul's unequivocal claim that the love of God in Jesus Christ is not only historic fact but the living, governing fact at the heart of the universe. That love will triumph over all things and it cannot be defeated or finally thwarted by any of the events of earth.

Very often men tend to regard such a statement as a rhetorical extravagance not to be taken too seriously, a piece of shallow optimism. But that is to misunderstand Paul, who was an adventurer as well as a theologian. He wrote out of a varied experience which included much hardship and adversity and as if to rebut this very criticism we so easily make, he ended this chapter by reciting his memorable catalogue of the foes we have to meet and then reiterating his claim that none of them can separate us from the love of God. Paul in fact is an undiluted optimist. 'To them that love God all things work together for good.'

At the other extreme we have the undiluted pessimism of Bertrand Russell who, after pondering the same facts as Paul, reaches this conclusion : 'Brief and powerless is man's life; blind to good and evil, reckless of destruction, omnipotent matter rolls on its relentless way . . . only, therefore, on the firm foundation of unyielding despair can the soul's habitation be safely built.'

What are the grounds on which Paul based his triumphant conclusion? They would appear to be two :

(i) First of all, a recognition of human freedom and man's moral stature. Within limits man is free to choose the way of the soul's progress. He can move towards God or away from Him. This truth in itself emphasizes the love of God. Man's freedom is indeed fraught with perilous consequences, when misused, but it is the measure of God's respect for human personality. God has created man capable of fellowship with Himself. God thought that a worthy purpose, and Himself accepted the consequence of His creative act. He does not withhold the gift He has bestowed, in spite of the ills which result from its misuse. Paul anticipated the scientists of today when he declared : 'We know that the whole creation groaneth and travaileth together in pain until now, waiting for the revealing of the sons of God.'

The significance and the worthwhileness of life reside in the individual and especially in the choices he makes. This delivers a man from the tyranny of circumstance. It never really matters in the end what happens to anybody, though that looms so large at the time. The important thing is how we react to what happens. Nothing at all can happen from which we may not pluck a blessing. These experiences are the raw material out of which we ourselves are fashioned, and the vital question is what kind of people we are becoming as a result of these experiences. Are we becoming sons of God or educated brutes? 'To them that love God all things work together for good.' Such a man does not need to select certain experiences, but he has learned to resent no discipline and to evade no task. He does not need to turn a blind eye to certain things and set his teeth grimly in the face of others. Everything that happens can bring with it a blessing, as, by the same token, to them that love not God—all things work together for evil. Neither success nor failure, neither sunshine nor rain, neither life nor death can bring with it anything of abiding worth.

(ii) The second great fact which justifies Paul's faith is the fact of divine grace. By grace in this sense is meant all those divine activities whereby in love God seeks to achieve His creative purpose.

God Himself is outside and greater than all the processes by which that purpose is worked out. By His grace He has bestowed on us the material blessings of life. By the same grace He has endowed us with spiritual gifts and made possible for us life in fellowship with Him. When we misuse His gift of freedom, when we sin against His holy will and reject His gracious approaches, we experience poverty instead of plenty, misery instead of joy. But the grace of God is available for us still. Our Lord Jesus Christ, though He was rich yet for our sakes became poor, that we through His poverty might become rich. Though we were yet sinners, Christ died for us. God Himself in all the plenitude of grace entered into our life, accepted all the consequences of our sin, and remained true to the way of divine love to the end. So even man's wrath is turned to His praise. The very cross itself, symbol of shame, is transfigured with glory and is the emblem of the victory which overcomes the world, proclaiming to all men for all time that there is nothing at all which cannot minister to God's holy purpose of love.

As we, helpless in our sin, respond to that love of God in Jesus Christ, we receive His grace which forgives us and then enables us to become, through Him, victors in the moral struggle, conquering where before we fell. Our lives become rooted deeper than circumstances and we become persuaded, not as an article of faith, but as a living experience, that 'neither death, nor life, nor angels, nor principalities, nor things present, nor things to come, nor powers, nor height, nor depth, nor any other creature, shall be able to separate us from the love of God which is in Christ Jesus our Lord'.

5

The Doctrine of Man

WE preachers are sometimes accused of dealing with themes with which the man in the pew, let alone the man in the street, is not interested. Who has not heard complaints that the sermon was remote from the lives and problems of ordinary men and women? It is difficult to see how such complaints could be justified or even arise when the theme is that with which we are concerned in this article. Many people seem to go through life without thinking much about *God*, though one would not expect to find such among our congregations. There can scarcely be any, even among the least reflective, who are not troubled these days about *man*. 'What is man?' enquired the Psalmist more than two thousand years ago, and his query is echoed on all sides today. For man, who has solved so many problems of the universe in this generation, ironically enough seems baffled by the problem of himself. From one point of view, of course, the answer can be given with greater certainty than ever before. The long process of evolution whereby man has reached his present state has been brilliantly investigated and in consequence man knows more about his origin than ever before. But he knows less about his destiny. He is unsure of himself and has lost faith in his fellow men. That is true at the individual level, but it is equally true of larger groups, such as classes and nations. This has led to chaos in the realm of conduct, especially in men's relation with each other. Men are uncertain as to the true way of life and have completely failed to solve the problem of living together. Nor is there any hope of better things, until the question of man's true nature and life's real purpose is settled in a way which will win assent and command allegiance.

To this fundamental question Christianity offers the one satisfying answer, and there is no more fruitful preaching today than that which meets this widespread need. From a score of different angles we should be hammering away to drive home this truth. Let me set it forth in a way which will, I hope, suggest some lines of approach.

The Christian doctrine of man is derived from the Christian doctrine of God. It is in terms of God's character and purpose as revealed in Jesus that we understand man's nature. We are not concerned to deny the accredited results of man's scientific research into his own origin; but we do affirm that that is of secondary importance. About almost everything, two questions may be asked, the question 'How?' and the question 'Why?' The question 'How?' is interesting and it is usually the scientist's business to answer it. The question 'Why?' is vital and is outside the field of science. The deepest truth about man is that he is created by God and is the object of God's care and love in a unique way. He has been created in God's image (Genesis 1²⁷), and the thing about him, which marks him out as distinct from the rest of God's creation, is not his intelligence but his moral and spiritual capacity. Only men can know that God made them, only men are addressed by Him and capable of responding to Him. Only men have another scale of values than things which can be seen and measured; only men can be tormented by what is called conscience.

It is in the light of this truth of man's kinship with God that we can best drive home the awful fact of sin. As only man can respond to God, so also only man can withhold that response. The fact that he has done so stares us in the face in the world round about us, and all of us come under this condemnation. While the fall of man is in one sense the supreme tragedy of the universe, it is also, as G. K. Chesterton loved to remind us, a doctrine full of hope. Animals can't fall. Humpty Dumpty could fall but never rise again. Man can and does fall, but he belongs essentially to God, and the gospel of God's love is the good news of how man may be restored to his high estate. For this to happen the first pre-requisite is that man shall recognize his sin and be aware of his utter need of God's grace. Not to have a sense of sin, far from being a cause of satisfaction, should fill us with dismay, for it suggests we are deficient in that moral sense which is a cardinal attribute of genuine humanity.

We saw in an earlier chapter how belief and behaviour are linked together. So it is essential that when we preach about practical questions of right conduct—as we certainly ought to do—we should remind our hearers that the character of God is the only ultimate sanction of all morality. If the world came into being by accident and there is no divine will and purpose in which our lives have a place, right and wrong become a mere matter of convenience. But right is right, not because it makes for greatest good of the greatest number, though that is true, but because the world is ruled by God who is Himself the source of all goodness. Wrong is wrong, not because it brings disaster and distress to ourselves and others, though that is also true, but because it is rebellion against the living God, who made us and to whom we must render account.

A sermon advocating temperance or opposing war is lifted on to a different plane, if it is explicitly related to the Christian doctrine of man. Otherwise what should be a prophetic utterance becomes merely an improving homily.

Our Lord's example in this matter is before us. He was never tired of reminding men that they should live as 'sons of the Father', and the supreme standard he set forth, which sums up all the rest, is that we should be perfect, for the one sufficient and indeed compelling reason that God is perfect and we are His children.

6

The Advent Hope

THE beginning of the Christian year is not Christmas, but the first Sunday in Advent, four or five weeks beforehand. It is part of the genius of Christianity that before we look back across the centuries to the coming of our Lord in great humility, we are bidden to look forward to His second coming in glory to judge both the quick and the dead. This Christian hope is an inseparable part of our heritage. It is enshrined in our hymns (e.g. *M.H.B.* 257, 264, etc.), it is enshrined in the historic creeds of the church, and it is enshrined in the Communion Service when we 'show forth the Lord's death till He come'.

What are we to make of it in our thinking and in our preaching? It must be confessed that to the average Christian it means little or nothing and finds no real place in his working faith.

First of all, let us look briefly at the history of this belief and see how it got its place and why it waned and lost its hold. It is clear that the belief dominated the thought of the earliest Christians. The earliest writings in the New Testament are the epistles of St. Paul who was aptly described by the late Quiller-Couch as 'the apostle of Jesus Christ, crucified, risen and *to come*'. Those to whom Paul wrote lived in daily expectation of the second coming of their Lord. That may well account for the fact that the gospels were not written for some years afterwards.

There was to be only a short interval between the end of the gospel events and the end of the world as we know it. How far if at all our Lord Himself shared this view is a matter on which scholars are not agreed. One thing is clear. The belief in no way affected His moral teaching, as some have urged, for the basis of that teaching is the character of God, and is not affected one whit by the considerations of the duration of what we call human history. Furthermore, we need to bear in mind that the idea of progress is quite modern in its conception. It is difficult for us to put ourselves into the position of people without that idea, but we must make the attempt. If they thought that the human story was to have a culmination, they had perforce to think of it in catastrophic terms, and clothe the idea in pictorial imagery. So it was that they looked for another divine invasion of human life when the victorious Christ would return and the Day of Judgement would dawn.

The main reason for the waning of the belief was simply that it didn't happen. Christians began to die and that in itself became a problem for their thinking. Paul himself laid less and less stress on the doctrine. If we arrange his letters in the order in which they were written we can see how true that is, though the belief never entirely disappeared from his writing. At the end he became quite reconciled to the idea that he himself would die first. The belief was revised in the light of the facts. This life must still be regarded as an interval before the great finale but the interval was now of indefinite length. A re-examination of the teaching of Jesus revealed the fact that the part of His teaching that was most original and characteristic had little to do with this belief, and this fact appeared very clearly in the Fourth Gospel, written later than the others, in which references to the Second Coming occupy a very subordinate position. The belief has never entirely disappeared, and there are always some who nurture the expectation in its most materialistic form at the heart of their Christian belief. This is especially so when conditions in the world are desperate and men give up hope of finding a way out.

What part is this advent hope to play in our preaching? Most of us probably feel that there is no reason to suppose that our Lord will come on the clouds of heaven in our own lifetime any more than in any of the generations that have preceded us. That is one of the things that must be left to God's own time. We are powerless to hasten or delay it. No man knoweth the day or the hour. But does that mean that we have to discard the whole doctrine as an exploded fallacy or at any rate as something that is not our practical concern? Assuredly not. Something invaluable which is bound up with the core and essence of our faith would thus be lost. It is our business to proclaim the positive truths which the doctrine safeguards.

Let me briefly mention two such truths which seem to me of supreme importance. First, there is the recognition that history is an unfolding drama. Something is happening in this life. A real battle is being fought out and there will be an end. Life is not meaningless. Its meaning is revealed in the historic drama of the life, death, and resurrection of Jesus. Now there is an interval, a long interval maybe, but an interval, a period during which the triumph of Christ has to work itself out on the stage of history, which can only be understood in the light of God's revelation of Himself in Jesus. Every crisis in individual lives or in the wider realm of affairs is related to that revelation of God's eternal purpose. The end will be not in time but in eternity. God's purpose may be delayed but never frustrated. This is our Christian faith in contrast to those totalitarian faiths which hold that some earthly state can afford an adequate goal for human endeavours. The history of the Ages, we believe, will be summed up in Jesus Christ. Every one of us is a pilgrim towards that goal, and all history will be caught up in the great fulfilment of God's purpose.

The other cardinal Christian truth, which the doctrine of

the Second Coming safeguards is the fact of Judgement.
This truth is vividly portrayed in many of our Lord's parables
in the first and third gospels. There will be a final reckoning.
In the Fourth Gospel the idea of judgement as an ever
present fact is stressed and developed. In that sense every
day is a coming of Christ. We are all of us in process of
becoming and every choice we make plays its part in deciding
the movement of our lives to their ultimate destiny. This
fact has its grim aspect which I would not attempt to deny,
but it is a part of the great Christian hope. It is because
we are judged that we may also be saved. What we are
matters to God. He is concerned with our conduct and our
character. So He judges us. In the light of that truth we
may receive and respond to His offer of salvation and know
Jesus, who is our Judge, as our Saviour and our Lord.

He came long years ago in Bethlehem where the love and
wisdom of God were incarnate in a Baby. To that coming
we look back in adoration and thanksgiving. He will come
again at the last day, when He shall take His power and
reign. To that we look forward with hope. But He comes
today and every day to judge and to save.

Where meek souls will receive Him, still
The dear Christ enters in.

7

Palm Sunday

EACH of the great Christian festivals has its own distinctive
appeal. For many people there is no time like Christmas,
the festival of purity and joy. This is the time when children's eyes grow bright, when even the most pre-occupied
catch strains of heavenly music. For believers it is thrilling
to meet around the manger at Bethlehem and sing carols of

the mystery of God's love. It is idle, however, to pretend that the Christmas story had no sequel or that we can pause indefinitely at that point in the calendar of our remembrance. The most casual reflection serves to remind us that a manger was a hard place to sleep in and that the baby who lay there was later crucified on Calvary.

For others, Easter is the greatest of all festivals. There is no more holy time than Easter morning when in every land on earth the faithful raise their Hallelujahs and greet their risen Lord at the table where He appoints. The message of Easter meets man's deepest need. It proclaims the victory won for us by Divine love in the very citadel of evil, and assures us that in this world of blood and iron the victory remains with love. It tells of joy through pain and of life through death. At Easter we celebrate the victory He won long years ago and we anticipate by faith His final triumph. But, if we may not linger for ever round the manger, equally surely we may not dwell without interruption on the glories of Easter. We see not yet all things subject to Him. The battle He won once for all has to be fought out on the stages of history and in all our hearts.

To realize this is to appreciate the significance of Palm Sunday, a festival we tend to neglect. To the Christian preacher Palm Sunday brings an unequalled opportunity of presenting vividly the challenge of Jesus to men and women and to the world. It is a pity that so often this opportunity is lost because Passion music takes the place of the sermon on this occasion. By all means let the message of the Cross be conveyed by music, but, if possible, on some other occasion than Palm Sunday evening.

On Palm Sunday the issues are so plain and our Lord's challenge to His people is clear. He intended that it should be so, for that day witnessed the beginning of the third and final stage in His ministry.

The first stage was that of the Galilean morning when Jesus came proclaiming the Kingdom of God and calling on men to repent and believe the Gospel. It was a time of popular enthusiasm when the common people flocked to hear Him. It was the period of the miracles of healing and compassion. Before long it became clear to Him that the multitude was attracted to Him by the wrong motive and that He could not achieve His end that way. Moreover, in certain quarters hostility to His mission developed on the part of those who were disappointed that He did not fit in to their ready-made programmes. Plots against His life were laid which, if allowed to mature, would at the very least have brought this first stage to an end in the wrong way and before He was ready.

Accordingly our Lord withdrew from the public eye for a time and devoted Himself to training His disciples for the work which one day would be theirs. Of necessity we know comparatively little of this stage, which reached its climax at Caesarea Philippi, when our Lord won from His disciples through the mouth of St. Peter their confession of His Messiahship.

The time for talking is now past and the time for action has arrived. Our Lord came out again into the open and ' steadfastly set His face to go to Jerusalem '. We do not know the precise time at which the shadow of the cross fell on our Lord's pathway, but there can be no doubt that He knew on Palm Sunday what would befall Him. Knowing all that was involved, He deliberately threw down the gauntlet to His foes. Many others, like Socrates or like faithful soldiers, have been willing to die; Jesus was determined to die. The choice lay between going on to an end that was now inevitable, or abandoning His mission. Jesus went on and in such a way as to make clear for all time the significance of what was happening.

He chose the time, the Feast of the Passover, when Jerusalem would be full of pilgrims from all parts. He chose the place, Jerusalem, the headquarters of the nation's civil, political and religious life; Jerusalem, the Holy City, heir to all the promises. He chose the symbolism and set Himself to fulfil in detail the prophecy of Zechariah as to the manner in which the Messiah would come. All this He did that those with insight would appreciate the significance of His claim.

Thus on Palm Sunday Jesus rode into Jerusalem to claim the throne. We call it ' The Triumphal Entry '. But He did not ride on a war-horse, like a Roman general returning from the wars, with a procession of captives behind His chariot. A donkey, the beast of burden, bore Him towards Jerusalem and the crowd scattered palm branches and garments in His path.

So the stage is set and the wheel of events set in motion which moved to its dreadful climax on Good Friday.

Here surely is a theme by means of which the challenge of our Lord can be brought home to the most careless listeners ! I would suggest that the introduction to the Palm Sunday sermon might be an attempt to portray in some such fashion, as has been done here, the dramatic significance of this moment in the Passion story. From that every preacher in his own way will apply the story to his hearers and to our world. Let the hearers feel themselves part of that crowd which went before and followed after. For we all have our place in that crowd. There were the enthusiastic who cried 'Hosanna ! ' some of whom at any rate were among those who after only a few days shrieked ' Crucify ! ' So fickle is human popularity and so easily swayed are those whose faith has no firm foundation. There were political and religious vested interests represented by well-intentioned men who saw their prerogatives threatened by this upstart Jesus, and who deluded themselves that they were acting in defence of Church and State. And there were disciples, torn between fear and joy, puzzled but yet following Him. One of these will betray Him, the most perfervid will deny Him, and all will in the end forsake Him. But they love Him and they follow. One day they will carry on His work and turn the world upside down. Meanwhile, they mingle with the crowd that acclaims Him as He rides into Jerusalem to claim the throne. Nineteen hundred years have passed, and the scene is changed. Yet it is ever the same. He still claims the throne of the world and of men's hearts. When we examine ourselves in honesty, what reply does He in fact receive from us?

8

The Doctrine of the Cross

I FIND this the most difficult chapter to write, not because there is little to say, but because there is so much. 'I determined not to know anything among you save Jesus Christ and him crucified' (1 Corinthians 2²). So Paul described the centrality for him of the doctrine of the Cross. And central the Cross must surely be in all our preaching. For God's revelation of Himself to us in Jesus Christ is clearest of all on Calvary, where our Lord triumphantly completed His redemptive work.

There are certain things in life, and they are often the most important things, which we can best understand by looking at them rather than talking about them. The meaning of the Cross belongs to this category. Indispensable as words may be as a means of communication, some truths are best portrayed by pictures. It is not without significance that Isaac Watts' hymn—perhaps the greatest of all hymns about the Cross—begins 'When I survey the wondrous cross' and in my view Watts' instinct was a true one. If I were asked how best to explain the heart of our Christian religion to one entirely ignorant of its meaning, I could think of no better way than to lead him, if I could, to the green hill outside the City wall, and let him mingle with the crowd at the foot of the Cross and listen to the words that fall from the Saviour's lips—'Father, forgive them . . .' Thus would he enter more surely than as a result of any argument or explanation into the supreme mystery.

> *'Tis mystery all! let earth adore,*
> *Let angel minds inquire no more.*

Our Lord Himself met the need, not only of His disciples but of His followers for all time, when He enjoined that through the outward symbols of His broken body and His shed blood they should proclaim His death.

So I would urge that our supreme task as preachers in this respect is to invite our congregations ever and again to gather with us at the foot of the Cross. Let us employ all the skill God has given us to portray vividly the crucified Saviour, assured that, in so far as we succeed in this, He will evoke from our hearers the authentic response.

Many theories of the atonement have been propounded at different times by different theologians, and there is probably an element of truth in all of them; but we do well to remember for our comfort that the Church is committed to no particular theory, but to the fact of the atonement as a glorious experience open to all, however wise or however simple.

Are we then not to explain or seek to explain? Of course, we must explain as far as we are able. God has given us minds and there is no theme with which our minds should grapple more eagerly than this theme of God's salvation, so long as we have constantly in mind that all our explanations will fall short of the glorious truth and that no finite understanding can 'sound the depths of love divine'. But I would suggest that we content ourselves with dealing from time to time with different aspects of the truth and allow the Cross to shed its own light on whatever facet of evangelical truth we are seeking to illumine, rather than attempt at any one time to deliver a comprehensive exposition of the doctrine of the Cross.

Reflect for a moment on the great words of our faith— Forgiveness, Redemption, Atonement, Justification, Salvation. Is it not true that, from whatever angle we approach any of these great subjects, it is only in the light of the Cross that they can be effectively expounded? Or consider again the great problems that perplex men's minds and sometimes break their hearts, the problem of evil, the mystery of suffering, the workings of Divine Providence; we shall only succeed in bringing comfort and inspiration to men and women struggling with these questions in the context of their own lives as we help them to interpret their own experience in the light of the Cross of Jesus.

If this be true, I must adopt the same plan for the remainder of this chapter, for our purpose is not to arrive at some complete and satisfying explanation of our Lord's death, but to consider together some lines along which we can hope to present the great truths of our redemption to those who listen to us.

Let me then as an example suggest an approach which I myself have always found particularly helpful ever since I first heard it unfolded by our leader in a society class to which I belonged before entering the ministry. Across the years I have turned again and again to this and, as I myself have been so greatly helped by it, I venture to pass it on to you.

What is the personal issue with which the Atonement is concerned? It is the issue of *reconciliation*. Man as a result of sin is separate from God. This is always the consequence of sin. 'God was in Christ reconciling the world unto Himself' (2 Corinthians 5¹⁹). So through our Lord's death man's supreme need of at-one-ment with God is met. But how does this occur? Our Lord taught us to think of our relationship with God in terms of human relationships. We can best understand God's attitude to us by thinking of Him as Father. Accordingly, consider a situation where there is a breakdown of happy relations between a human father and his son. As a result of the boy's disobedience the happy confidence which should exist between them is broken. How is it to be restored? How can reconciliation be brought about? Three conditions require to be fulfilled. These are stated in order for purposes of clarity, but clearly they need not follow each other in strict succession.

(1) The father must indicate his willingness to forgive his son and receive him back into his confidence and favour. This is absolutely vital. How many breaches are never healed because the wronged person waits for the offender to take the first step. This is utterly mistaken. Most people who have wronged another are too ashamed of themselves to feel they have a right to a restoration of the happy relationship and would feel it presumptuous to suggest anything of the kind. Hence the initiative in such circumstances rests with the one who has suffered wrong.

(2) In taking the initiative the father must in no way condone or gloss over the evil that the son has committed. On the contrary, he must do everything possible to bring home the seriousness of the offence. No abiding and worthy reconciliation can take place unless the forgiven offender recognizes the reality and heinousness of his sin and renounces it.

(3) The father's initiative must be of such a kind as to kindle in the heart of his son a warmth of feeling whereby he will respond so gladly and freely that the breach is well and truly healed and the newly restored relationship firmly welded. It is in the atmosphere of mutual love that permanent reconciliation takes place.

Turning from our human analogy to God's redemptive love in Jesus Christ, we see how all these conditions are fulfilled.

(1) 'God was in Christ reconciling the world unto Himself'. The atonement takes place as a result of God's initiative. How different it would be if Paul had written 'Christ was in the world reconciling God and man'. But it is not so. Reconciliation is not effected as a result of what man intends or initiates. It springs from the heart of God, who does not wait for man to turn to Him in repentance, but seeks His

wandering children as the shepherd seeks the sheep that have strayed from the fold. The New Testament story is not the story of man groping after God, if haply he may find Him, but of God in Jesus Christ seeking and saving the lost. It is God who offers His gracious forgiveness, man who responds to God's love.

(2) No one who has accepted God's offer of forgiveness through Jesus Christ, and realized at what tremendous cost our Lord has redeemed us, is likely to treat sin as a light thing. It is in the light of the Cross of Jesus that we begin to understand the sinfulness of sin. When we remember that it was sin like ours which sent our Lord to the cross, it is the end of any casual attitude towards sin. We see there what our sins do to God as we see also how divine love deals with human sin.

(3) Finally, the testimony of countless Christians across the centuries is that it is wonder at what our Lord suffered for us on the Cross that has broken sin's hold over men and won their complete and glad response, whereby they have received power to renounce their sin and give themselves utterly to God in a renewed fellowship with Him which brings moral and spiritual victory and abiding peace.

> *Love so amazing, so divine,*
> *Demands my soul, my life, my all.*

9

Easter

IT is not difficult to understand the almost universal appeal of Easter. Men and women are incurably melodramatic. We like happy endings. Thomas Hardy, prophet of futility, may compel our admiration by his consummate artistry, but he does not win our hearts. We like books and plays and films where virtue emerges triumphant over all. We were enthralled as youngsters with the stories of beggarmaids who turned out to be princesses.

The world is full of such wonderful stories, many of them doubtless the same story in different forms. Often it takes the form that what seems the end is really another beginning; the story of Dionysus, the story of the phoenix, and so on. The ever-recurring miracle of Spring strikes a responsive chord in all our hearts and we feel it appropriate that the religious festival of Easter should be celebrated when all nature is proclaiming the message of life through death.

This very similarity brings its own danger. Congregations on Easter Sunday are usually considerably larger than on ordinary occasions, in spite of the fact that many regular worshippers avail themselves of the opportunity afforded by the first holiday of the year to snatch a brief vacation. Furthermore, although the practice of holding services in Holy Week and on Good Friday is increasing, the overwhelming proportion of those present on Easter Sunday will have attended no service since at any rate Palm Sunday. Consider what this means. The period between Palm Sunday and Easter Day will have been passed over unnoticed except by those who have dwelt on it in private prayer and reflection.

Then comes the Easter service with its ' hallelujahs ' and all the pageantry of triumph. In these circumstances it is desperately easy for the celebration of Easter to become shallow and superficial, altogether out of harmony with the faith of the first Easter. The Cross, if thought of at all, is something over and done with. The Lord is risen.

But this is entirely to misunderstand the meaning of Easter. One difference between the Easter story and the other stories I have referred to is that there was nothing melodramatic about it. It was characterized by amazing restraint. The risen Lord did not show Himself in triumph to His enemies. Pilate was not discomfited nor Herod confounded. If He had been willing to win allegiance by such means He would have done so long before. It was to those who were sad at

His departure, whose hopes were shattered but who still loved Him, that He came.

The effect of the resurrection on those earliest disciples was not to contradict what happened on Good Friday, but to vindicate and illumine it. The interval between was the time it took them to understand what had really happened. The Emmaus story shows us very clearly how our Lord helped them to do this. When they did understand they carried the Cross from which before they had fled.

The message of Easter is not the proclamation of life apart from death, but of life through death. The only road to Easter Day lies through Good Friday. As that was true for Him, so is it for the believer. ' I have been crucified with Christ,' declared Paul, ' therefore I live.' That is one note we preachers might well think it good to sound on Easter Day. Another approach which also has the merit of making the meaning of the festival utterly real, is to link our Lord's victory in time 1,900 years ago with the victory which we through Him can win over evil in our own hearts. It is not easy for our congregations, or even for us who preach, to put ourselves back into the position of the disciples on the first Good Friday. It is always difficult to recapture the emotions of a previous occasion. We all know on every Good Friday that in two days' time we shall be celebrating the Resurrection. But they did not know that.

On the first Good Friday friend and foe alike thought it was the end of Jesus. The difference was that, while His foes were relieved and gleeful, His friends were a scattered rabble, bedraggled survivors of a lost cause. Their Master was slain and His teaching about God revealed to be moonshine. Love had been vanquished with every attendant circumstance of ignominy. Then came the first Easter Day when the most glorious Lord of life came back, having burst the gates of hell and opened the Kingdom of Heaven to all believers. God had laid bare His mighty arm in a work of redemption comparable only to the morning of creation. The effect was revolutionary. The disorganized rabble became an army. The Church was born. Rising from their bemoaning, the disciples, with light in their eyes and their whole souls aglow, sprang on the world with the message of a risen Saviour.

As always in the New Testament, the victory of our Lord is a victory which can be reproduced in the believer. We live in a world where the things of the spirit often seem frail and fugitive compared with the ponderable things of the world. But the Christian is a risen man. The Resurrection is not an event in a remote and ever-receding past, but a present fact. It is something to which effective witness may be borne in our homes and in the office or factory where we work. Where before we lost we can now win. The victory He won in time, which is an anticipation of the final victory in eternity, is a victory He seeks to win in and through us now. Let two texts in conclusion suggest to us this line of approach to the Easter theme. 'If then ye were raised together with Christ, seek the things that are above, where Christ is' (Colossians 3[1]). 'One died for all, therefore all died; and He died for all that they which live should no longer live unto themselves, but unto Him, who for their sakes died and rose again' (2 Corinthians 5[14, 15]).

10

The Ascension

THE doctrine of the Ascension of our Lord does not usually receive the attention it deserves. We have noticed how many church-goers pass from Palm Sunday to Easter with no public acknowledgement of Good Friday. But it may be fairly urged that at any rate they all know about Good Friday and give it some place in their private thoughts. When it comes, however, to Ascension Day, which always falls on a Thursday, it is to be feared that a large proportion of practising Free

Churchmen allow the festival to pass entirely unnoticed. Nor is this omission by any means invariably corrected in the services on the following Sunday. This is a great pity, as the doctrine of the Ascension should be to us a real source of comfort and strength. The remedy, in part at any rate, is in the hands of us who preach and I would suggest that, if we find ourselves planned on the Sunday after Ascension, we should seek to expound the meaning of the festival to our hearers.

In this connexion let us not overlook the great Ascension hymns, notably 'The head that once was crowned with thorns' and 'Away with gloom, away with doubt!', the latter of which is one of the most splendid modern hymns on this subject.

There are difficulties about this doctrine, one of the chief of which is that the very idea of our Lord's Ascension seems remote. We have been following His story from the cradle to the cross, all those events which took place in this world of space and time, and which came to their glorious climax in the Resurrection, and now we come to an event which seems to remove the interest to another sphere with which we have little to do at present. What practical bearing can this have on the day-to-day lives of ordinary men and women, what bearing on this world of woes and disasters, of hatred and suffering? Furthermore, after 1900 years the story itself presents difficulties. Heaven is spoken of as a geographical location and God described in human terms as having a right hand.

Well, let us look at it. A good way to begin is to realize first what the event meant to the disciples themselves. All the Gospels agree that after His crucifixion, the Risen Lord returned from death to life and was seen by His disciples. There is an element of mystery surrounding those appearances, inevitable when we consider the uniqueness of the event. Our Lord appeared only at intervals and was not subject to the ordinary limitations which apply to men and women. The

Ascension is the story of the last of such manifestations. It was not only the last, but they knew that it was the last. He had now withdrawn into the unseen world whence He had come. In Jesus the Eternal had entered into time—

> Our God contracted to a span,
> Incomprehensibly made man.

That revelation in time was now at an end. This fact, unlike His first departure on Good Friday, filled them with joy. They were alone in Jerusalem, which had become a deathtrap for the followers of Jesus—but they were not alone. He was with them in a more real way than He ever could be in the flesh, and their mood was one of triumph, not of defeat.

So for us the Ascension might be termed the Festival of the unseen but real world. No fact is more important than that the unseen things are the real things. If that is not true, all values are changed and man is doomed to corruption and death. The meaning of the universe, we believe, is spiritual. The most wonderful things in life are not the things we can see or touch, weigh or measure, the most wonderful and the most real things are the unseen values, such as truth, friendship, goodness and love. These can and should be expressed in visible things, but they themselves are invisible. The material things are only the scaffolding and preparation for the building, which is spiritual.

When a man goes into his room and shuts his door and prays to his Father in Heaven, when he allows some imponderable factor to sway him so that he rejects some material gain for an ideal, when he quenches his natural resentment and forgives an injury, he is paying tribute to the reality of what cannot be seen. It is man's glory that, unlike the animals, he is capable of striving after what has not yet come about. When he does so he interprets himself and the meaning of life in terms of those haunting visions of the Divine which never leave us. Of this primacy of the unseen, the Ascension of Jesus is a graphic symbol and a perpetual reminder. So for the disciples the Ascension signified not the absence of their Lord but the presence and reality of the unseen world. It was not that Jesus was further from them but that heaven was nearer to them. Surely that is the Christian way to think of the departure of our loved ones in the faith. Each of them is another strong link binding us to that unseen and eternal world.

Following on from that we see that our Lord's Ascension means that He is the centre of that real world, which is to be interpreted by Him. It is a tremendous and inspiring thing to ponder ever and again the great historic facts of God's revelation in Jesus. It is an even greater thing to believe and know that one day all things shall be summed up in Him. That is what the Ascension means. 'The suffering dying Jesus is the Christ upon the Throne.' The Easter victory is more than an episode; it is an anticipation in time of His final victory when He shall put all things under His feet. When He came in great humility there was no room for Him in the world, because He would not fit in with the schemes of man, but only God's plan will in the end fit the world. That is the perspective of the Christian. We are passing through a world of time and space to a life where things eternal take the place of the things of time. We live and plan and have our day, but He has wrought for us an eternal redemption. His is by right the Kingdom and the power and the glory, and ours is the victory through Him because all that is His is ours.

11

Temptation

WHEN a preacher chooses Temptation as his theme, he has the great advantage of dealing with a subject which is familiar to all his hearers. Whatever the composition of the audience, be they young or old, male or female, rich or poor, temptation

will form part of their experience. When our Lord under-
went this experience, He was one with all the human race
for, though we men differ from one another in so many
ways, we are alike in this, that moral conflict is the order
under which we live. How men regard temptation will
depend largely on their mood at the moment. 'Count it all
joy when ye fall into manifold temptation' is the counsel of
one New Testament writer, and we may indeed rejoice that
this experience, like all experiences, is one from which a
blessing may be plucked. Temptation may be victoriously
overcome, and when that is so, the soul is stronger for the
experience and better fitted for the next onslaught of the
adversary. That does not mean, however, that temptation
should be coveted for the benefit it may bring. Any man
who is sensitive to the sinfulness of sin and realizes even in a
small degree at what a cost our redemption has been wrought,
will recoil from temptation rather than welcome it. It is one
thing to glory in the power of God to succour us, but quite
another to approach the conflict lightheartedly or with
arrogant bravado. It is surely no accident that in the Lord's
Prayer the petition 'Lead us not into temptation' follows the
prayer for the Divine forgiveness we all need.

We may well begin by asking our hearers to recognize that
temptation is inseparable from the life of people like us,
endowed as we are with the ability to distinguish between
right and wrong and continually faced with the responsibility,
terrible but glorious, of making moral choices.

We may further remind them that this sense of right and
wrong is one way in which God speaks to us and one out-
standing difference marking out men from the rest of creation.

From this starting point there are many lines of thought
we may profitably follow, among which the following suggest
themselves.

(1) Temptation is not sin. It is a call to battle. It is
part and parcel of the life we have to live. Otherwise our
Lord were the chief of sinners, but we read of Him that He

was 'tempted in all points even as we are, yet without sin'
To yield is sin, but not to be tempted. This point is well
worth making because, though it is so simple and clear, it is
far from being realized by everybody. Consequently many
people keep their temptations secret as something to be
ashamed of. It is natural, though by no means right, that
we should do this with our sins, but to do it with our temptations also is to deprive ourselves of the help God can give
us through one another. If the tempter can persuade us that
the conflict within us is a private war between us and him
he has succeeded in isolating us and has placed us at a
serious disadvantage. The truth is that the battle we are
waging is one in which all brave spirits everywhere play their
part, one indeed in which our Lord Himself has already won
the victory.

(2) In the experience of temptation the attack may well
come from without, but the issue is decided within our own
souls. How true this is, is seen from the fact that, though
everybody is tempted, no two people are tempted in exactly
the same way. Temptation takes different forms for different
people.

> *I see the sights that dazzle,*
> *The tempting sounds I hear.*

That is true of us all, but they are not the same sights that
dazzle us all, nor the same sounds we all hear.

The tempter's modes of approach are legion. He knows
our weak points, but is subtle enough often to assail us where
we think we are strong. Temptation comes to us along the
line of our own make-up, our ambition, our talents, our
careers. So it was that our Lord was tempted along the line
of His unique personality and mission. 'If thou be the Son
of God, command that these stones be made bread.' Our
Lord was tempted to gain His end by unworthy means.

It is the potential traitor within our own souls that constitutes our real danger. If we win the battle there, we need

ear no outward assault. But, if we lose there, the citadel
s betrayed from within and cannot stand.

(3) From this it is clear that the only way to meet tempta-
ion is by strengthening our souls within. Here is the point
of attack, here also must be the defence. Much has been said
of late concerning the need for self-expression. But surely
what matters is having a self fit to be expressed. Self-mastery
would seem a worthier aim. This is not to plead for unnatural
repression, but rather for a positive dedication of ourselves
to what is good, indeed to God in Jesus Christ. The secret
of our Lord's spiritual victory lay in His unswerving loyalty
to His Father's will. This carried Him through all temptation, even the last in the Garden of Gethsemane.

As we respond to God's love in Jesus Christ, that love takes
us and guards us. Not all the wiles of the devil can separate
us from it.

12

The Problem of Suffering

SOONER or later most, if not all, of us who preach feel bound
to deal with the problem of suffering. Similarly I have felt
that if these articles are to continue, the question would have
to be faced here. The reason for this is that the problem
constitutes one of the most dramatic challenges to the
Christian interpretation of life. Moreover, it affects everybody to a greater or less degree, either directly or through
those whom they love.

In spite of that, most of us feel a measure of hesitation in
preaching on this theme, as I do in writing about it. The
reason for this, as far as I personally am concerned, is that,
though a measure of suffering has come my way, I have not
yet been called on to bear an undue share; and further, when
physical suffering has been my lot, I have been neither patient
nor brave. Another reason for hesitation, and one that affects

everybody, is that we cannot hope to give our congregations a completely satisfying answer to a problem which constantly perplexes men's minds and sometimes breaks their hearts. We need to be on our guard against the temptation to talk glibly and utter empty platitudes. We must approach the theme with deep reverence lest we only aggravate the distress we seek to relieve.

Many books have been written which we might do well to read. Among them I would mention *The Problem of Pain* by C. S. Lewis, the well-known Oxford don, whose writings, since his conversion from unbelief, have contributed impressively to the defence of the Christian faith in general and to whose insight my own thoughts on this particular theme owe much.

It is scarcely necessary to add that in what follows, no attempt is made at an adequate or comprehensive treatment. Such is not the purpose of these articles anyhow, and would be especially absurd when dealing in so short a space with a subject like this. The aim is rather to throw out suggestions of various kinds, indicating possible lines of thought which may be developed in different ways.

To begin with, I find it helps to keep the problem in proportion and affords real relief to the mind to remember that suffering cannot be measured by amount. Suffering is not an idea but an experience. Vague talk about ' the colossal sum of human suffering' clouds the issue. The amount of suffering is limited by what any individual can experience. It is quite misleading, for example, to add my toothache to yours and other people's and so arrive at an aggregate amount of toothache in the world.

Next, and more importantly, the problem is only a problem at all because we believe in God as righteous and loving. If the universe is the creation of a devil or the result of blind chance, there is no problem. Suffering is then just a regrettable phenomenon to be avoided as far as we can. It is our Christian faith which is the awkward fact. Recognizing as

we do that suffering is native to humanity, we Christians none
the less proclaim the good news of the love of God. Our
task is to reconcile this with the experience of suffering which
is in some degree the lot of us all.

How can this be? Part of the answer undoubtedly is that
suffering is one way in which God's beneficent dealings with
us operate. Much human suffering springs directly from
man's misuse of the gift of freedom. Man is free to defy
God, but he cannot do this with impunity. Sin begets
suffering. When I sin, I am the first to suffer, but many
others may be involved in the suffering my sin causes. If it
were not so, one might indeed impugn God's providential
government of the world. Just as pain in the body is a signal
that something is amiss and requires attention, so the suffering
which is consequent upon man's sin shatters the illusion that
all is well. God is more concerned that we should be good
than that we should be comfortable, and in His discipline
suffering becomes, as Mr. Lewis describes it, 'a flag of truth
planted within a rebel fortress'. So the suffering attendant
upon war, for example, reminds us of the moral and spiritual
breakdown of which war is an outward sign. It is terrible,
but it would be more terrible if it were otherwise. 'Whom
the Lord loveth, He chasteneth.'

While this reflection affords a valuable clue to our understanding of the problem, it cannot be regarded as a complete
explanation. Sometimes suffering arises from causes entirely
outside our control, and further, we are so bound up with one
another that we suffer for one another's sins as well as for
our own, the innocent for the guilty. While much of this
must remain a mystery, we do well to bear constantly in mind
that, though suffering cannot be entirely explained, it can be
overcome. Often it makes men bitter, but by no means
always. If it leads on occasion to a conviction of God's
absence, it may also be a place where God meets us with His
enabling and redeeming grace. All of us know men and
women of whom this is true. The supreme example is our

Lord Himself of whom the writer to the Hebrews says that He ' learned by the things that He suffered' and that He was made ' perfect through sufferings '. We are disciples of One who in utter obedience to His Father took on Him the burden of the sin of the world and trod the path of suffering through mazes where God's purpose, and even His presence, was obscured by pain. His sufferings have done more than anything else in the world to win men from sin and error. He did not hesitate to invite His followers to tread the same road, in faith that all the powers of darkness will finally be overthrown by triumphant suffering love.

13

The Sin of Pride

OUR business as preachers is to proclaim the Gospel, the good news of God's redeeming love for undeserving sinners. Of our need to equip ourselves in every possible way we must constantly remind ourselves. Doubtless we are often conscious of our shortcomings in this respect.

There is, however, another obstacle to the effectiveness of preaching. This resides not in the preacher, but in the congregations we address. It is recorded of our Lord that on occasions He concluded His preaching with the injunction ' He that hath ears to hear, let him hear '. The equivalent of that in present day parlance would be ' This means you '. And I imagine that some such reminder would not be out of place in many of our churches today. We preachers sometimes sit in the pew and we know how fatally easy it is for us to listen to a sermon and think what an admirable sermon it is for somebody else to hear.

There are times in the open-air, for example, when we have the opportunity of reaching those to whom the Christian message is indeed ' news '—that is, it is something they really didn't know before, and that may always be true of a proportion of our hearers. But in most of our congregations there are many to whom the message is not 'news'. They know it already, and we are not likely to tell them anything that is entirely fresh. Our task with them is so to present what they already know as to convince them of its urgent relevance to them at this very moment for their own salvation. That is to say, we need to awaken in those who are listening to us a sense of their own present need of the grace of God.

It has been remarked that in the last analysis all sin is human pride setting itself against God. It would not be difficult to illustrate that today on a world scale, when we are witnessing a gigantic attempt on the part of humanity to save the world without God's help and largely in defiance of Him. But it is equally true at the personal level, as the New Testament abundantly demonstrates. 'God resisteth the proud but giveth grace to the humble' (1 Peter 5[5]), is a truth which runs right through the epistles. The young Christian communities addressed by Paul needed constantly to be reminded of it. Instances too numerous to be cited leap to all our minds. They may be summed up in the utter condemnation pronounced on the Church at Laodicea in the third chapter of the Book of the Revelation.

That this sin was the chief obstacle to the saving work of the Holy Spirit among those who had already made an initial response to the Christian message is not surprising when we turn to the Gospels and discover that it was also our Lord's chief difficulty in winning a hearing at all. Acknowledged sinners heard Him gladly and no-one turned to Him in vain. But He seemed to make no impression at all on the Pharisees, precisely because in their pride they lacked a sense of need. The Gospel is an offer of healing to those who know they are sick, a message of salvation to those who know they are in jeopardy. But the Pharisee knew neither of these things.

One of the ways in which Jesus sought to overcome this obstacle was by telling stories by means of which He hoped

4

to hold up a mirror to them in which they might see themselves and be jolted out of their complacency. Let us look briefly at three of them. The most obvious perhaps is the familiar parable of the Pharisee and the Publican. Here the point to notice is that by every recognized standard of conduct the Pharisee does indeed compare favourably with the publican. He was not a hypocrite in the accepted sense of a bad man pretending to be good. His spiritual error was that he did compare himself with the publican and in consequence preened himself on his relative excellence. He had no sense of need and his prayer could not be heard. Indeed, he prayed ' with himself ' and not to God at all. If he had seen himself in the light of God's purity and goodness, his prayer would have been very different. The publican, overcome by a realization of his unworthiness, could receive the grace of God.

Similarly, the elder brother, in the Parable of the Prodigal Son, had in truth a much better record than his scapegrace brother. But unfortunately he knew it and based his claims on it. He had no share in the family joy not because everybody excluded him. On the contrary, his father besought him to enter. The door was open, but something in himself made it impossible for him to go in. His whole outlook rested on a theory of merit and reward which is quite alien to the family of God. It is strange how the character of the elder brother still wins the sympathy of many people, who feel he received a raw deal. This fact alone emphasizes the necessity of our constantly reminding our hearers that the Gospel is for sinners who know that they are sinners, and not for the respectable who know they are respectable.

The third story is the Parable of the Labourers which is almost identical with the Parable of the Prodigal Son, though in another guise. At first sight the complaint of the Labourers seems so utterly reasonable, like that of the elder brother. But that is only while we are blinded by worldly standards and strangers to the economy of the Kingdom of Heaven. The

Kingdom of Heaven is not inhabited by those who have earned their place there, but by unprofitable servants, with no merit of their own, for whom Jesus died.

14

The Christian Hope

WHEN Dr. Welch, at that time B.B.C. Director of Religious Broadcasting, delivered his memorable address to the Methodist Conference at Nottingham in 1945, one of the most striking things he said was that among the hundreds of sermons it had been his duty to read he could only recollect one which was specifically on the theme of Immortality. Here were a company of men drawn from all the churches given an opportunity, for many of them the only opportunity, of addressing millions of listeners. It might be presumed that they would choose as their subject what seemed to them of supreme importance. It was the more amazing when we remember that the years involved were the war years when the power of man to kill and destroy was unleashed and sudden death on the battlefield and at home was the dominant feature of the contemporary scene. Before condemning too hastily the preachers concerned, let us ask ourselves whether in our own preaching the Christian hope has occupied its rightful place. Most of us could probably claim that it has been an assumption underlying all we have said, but surely that is not enough. If this is a true doctrine, it needs to be proclaimed and expounded, and our neglect of it not only weakens our presentation of Christian truth at a vital point, but also leaves that sphere to be annexed by others, notably the spiritualists, who have not been slow to enter the field.

On this question of the future life, men can be divided into four groups—

(1) Those (e.g. the rationalists) who are sure there is no such thing.

(2) Those (e.g. the spiritualists) who are sure there is and protest to have proof of that.

(3) Those who have no settled convictions on the matter. They feel there may or may not be a hereafter, but anyhow the whole thing is so vague and uncertain that the only thing to do is to make the best of this life and not bother about anything else.

(4) Those who, holding the Christian faith, believe in the resurrection of the dead and act accordingly.

In our congregations there are probably not many from categories (1) and (2), but, unless I am much mistaken, there are far too many who on this point are agnostics and come under category (3). Our business is to win from them a verdict as a consequence of which they will definitely be in category (4).

There seem to me to be three main reasons which together make it imperative that the preaching of immortality should be given again the prominent place it once had, but in recent years seems to have lost. Let me briefly state them in turn.

The first reason is simply that *this is a subject which is bound to engage the attention of everybody.* If a man takes life at all seriously, he can't help thinking about the hereafter, and if he doesn't take life seriously he can't help it in the end. Death is one of the governing facts of life. It is one of the few things we can be certain about in this uncertain world. All human life inevitably comes to an end. It is sometimes suggested that it is selfish to be concerned with it. Be that as it may, I venture to think that there are few of us who don't sometimes ask the question ' What will happen to me? ' Even if it were to be admitted that it is nobler not to be so concerned, how many of us attain such nobility, and anyway are we sure it is noble? Nor should it be assumed that it is only our own immortality we are concerned about. What about our loved ones? Their life is as brief and uncertain as our own and there is surely nothing selfish in thinking about them. However, that may be, the point is we can't help it, and that affords the preacher his opportunity. In dealing with this theme he can be assured of attentive hearers.

The second reason is that *we cannot really separate the problems of this life from those of the hereafter.* Here, I think, we find at any rate a partial explanation of the neglect of this type of preaching of late. There seems little doubt that there was a period when Christians in preaching and practice alike so concentrated on the next world that they ignored the rightful claims of this one. We are all familiar, no doubt, with hymns no longer sung where the emphasis is so completely of this kind that it would appear that those who sang them regarded life in this world as a regrettable necessity to be endured with as little inconvenience as possible. We shall agree that that must be wrong. Our life here must have a real place in God's purpose for us; otherwise it is difficult for us to understand why we should have been put here. Such an attitude was altogether unreal and merited the gibe of 'otherworldliness', uttered at its expense by many. But now the pendulum has swung to the other extreme. Taunted by its foes for its lack of social conscience, the Church tended to become absorbed by the problems of earth and to concentrate on this life as an end in itself. But this emphasis is equally unbalanced and must finally prove disastrous. It is an error into which Communism falls, and one irreconcilable difference between true Christianity and Communism. Communism teaches that the goal of all endeavour is a certain social order to be attained on earth. It leaves the hereafter entirely out of account. Let not Christians be guilty of this.

Christian truth holds the balance between these two extremes. Each of these extremes contains an element of truth, which is only seen in its true perspective when combined with the other.

If we regard this world as the be-all and end-all, if men and women are like machines wound up which are slowing down to an end which is only an end and not a new beginning, the individual soul is not worth very much in the sight of God, right and wrong have only a temporary significance and nothing really matters very much. But if, on the other hand, as Christians believe, this life is a porch leading to a fuller life, if the truth about man is that he is an immortal soul, and the purpose of his life here is to fit him for the hereafter, if his destiny hereafter is linked with his life here, the whole picture is transformed. No belief is more stimulating to the development of individual character, or exercises a more compelling influence for the transformation of society.

That then is the second reason for the importance of this doctrine. It is when we believe in immortality, not when we disbelieve in it or don't bother about it, that life here takes on its true urgency and significance.

The third reason is the most convincing of all. *If this doctrine goes, the whole edifice of Christian faith crumbles to bits.* There are Christian doctrines which are important but which could be thrown overboard without the whole structure collapsing, but not this one. Whatever else the Christian gospel does, it faces the fact of death, and proclaims its message about it. When any of us preaches, he preaches as a dying man to dying men. As a matter of history, that is how Christianity began. It was the resurrection of Jesus, His conquest of sin *and death* which gave the Christian movement its initial impetus. The last article of the creed ' and the life everlasting ' is also the crown of the creed. Salvation is salvation here and now but also in eternity. ' This is the promise which He promised us, even the life which is eternal '. The gift of God is eternal life. This is the significance of what God did 1900 years ago. This is the splendid structure of the Christian faith. The Eternal came into time, lived, died and rose again, not in order that we might be reconciled to Him for a brief space, but for ever. The ordinances of Baptism and the Lord's Supper alike proclaim this. This is the Christian interpretation of history, which declares with Paul that all things will be summed up in Christ. Remove this belief and the Christian faith offers neither inspiration to the individual soul nor a clue to life's whole meaning and purpose.

'If a man die, shall he live again?' asked Job. For us Christians another question is involved—'Did Jesus really show us God's character and purpose?' Not only human hope, but the divine purpose is at stake, and the gospel we preach can only meet the need of men in this life on earth as it unfolds to them the reality of the life that is eternal.

With these reasons in our minds let us now address ourselves to the content of the Christian doctrine of immortality. When this subject is discussed, many questions arise which cannot possibly be dealt with in a broad survey of this kind. 'What do we mean by the resurrection of the body?' 'Is there a second chance for the unrepentant sinner?' 'What about those who lived before Jesus or who have never heard the Gospel?' 'Is everybody judged at death?' and so on. This article makes no attempt to deal with questions of that sort. I would strongly recommend preachers to read a full length book on the subject, of which probably the best and most satisfying available is Dr. John Baillie's *And the Life Everlasting*.

We must content ourselves with a statement of the general principles which should underlie our treatment of the subject, and I think we can perhaps see these principles most clearly when we set our Christian belief over against other theories. In the previous chapter I contrasted Christian believers with three other groups of people, two of which are at opposite poles in this matter, namely Rationalists, on the one hand, who are sure there is no such thing as the future life, and Spiritualists, at the other extreme, who are sure there is and profess to have proof of it. Let us see how Christianity differs from each of these in turn.

1. The view of the rationalists in this connection is that it is impossible for human personality to survive the shock of physical death. The mind, they say, is a product of the

brain and when the brain ceases all mental faculties cease too. What we call the soul is not only physical in origin, it is an inseparable part of the physical organism, so that bodily existence is essential for the life of the soul. Man is just a highly intricate and complicated machine. When the machine stops that is the end of him.

Now there is no proof that this is not so, unless we accept the evidence of the spiritualists, to which we will turn later, but what we must always remember is that there is no proof that it is so. To hold the rationalist point of view is as much a matter of faith as to hold the Christian belief in immortality. Reason does not prove the rationalist's case, nor, as I think, does it make it probable. The name 'rationalist' in this sense seems to be a misnomer. I would rather describe those who hold this view as 'materialists'.

Against this we Christians maintain that, while our belief in immortality is not susceptible of proof, it is much more reasonable, and indeed we would go so far as to say that life without it is irrational and absurd. In support of this much can be said. We are reluctant to believe that ultimately life is meaningless, yet it is difficult to see how that conclusion can be avoided if there is no hereafter. When, in an earlier article, we were considering the Christian doctrine of Man, we noticed man's innate craving for perfection. This is characteristic of man in relatively small matters, such as the cultivation of flowers or the architecture of buildings. But most of all it's true in the moral sphere. There is a divine discontent which leaves man dissatisfied with anything less than the best. This is one thing which marks man out from the animals. The greatest men are those who know they are pilgrims. They are not finished products, but in process of becoming something different, something better. If the rationalists are right, all these aspirations are doomed to disappointment. Man, with his superb intelligence, his ability to recognize and strive after the true and the good, just comes to an end when the machine runs down, unless that end is precipitated earlier by a microbe or a bomb. If this is true, of what avail the struggle? Our loftiest desires and purest visions are out of accord with reality. The universe has thrown up something nobler than itself.

The same must be said of man's social aspirations. From Plato to the present day man has striven for Utopia. His dreams have indeed been frustrated, but that is the whole point. Are they never to be realized? Man differs from the animals in his power to entertain and pursue such ideals, but again, if there is no hereafter, of what avail the struggle?

But whereas all these aspirations, personal and social, are bound to be thwarted, if the rationalists are right, in the Gospel they receive the seal of God's own intention and redemptive purpose. Perfection is the standard set before the Christian and in His demands our Lord is uncompromising and inexorable. Perfection, however, is not primarily a demand but an offer. It is the final gift of God to undeserving sinners, the crown of God's saving work in us, and, though this may never be arrived at on earth, we begin to enjoy here and now that new quality of life called in the New Testament 'eternal', which is theirs who experience within themselves the saving power of the Holy Spirit.

Similarly, the Kingdom of God takes shape whenever the rule of God is accepted by an individual or expressed in society, but that Kingdom's consummation is outside this world of space and time.

So we confidently claim that the Christian doctrine of immortality meets man's deepest personal and social needs, and that without that doctrine life itself is ultimately meaningless and irrational. This is the consistent view of the New Testament writers, especially Paul. Here we are in process of being saved, there we shall be what in God's purpose we are meant to be, through the grace of our Lord and Saviour Jesus Christ, who will work in us His perfect will and present us faultless before the throne of God, members of the redeemed family He is gathering around Himself.

2. There is only space to state quite briefly how our Christian faith differs from that of the spiritualists. The spiritualists are at the opposite extreme to the rationalists in that they affirm that life continues in the hereafter and claim to prove it by evidence.

All must recognize the poignant facts of human experience which lead men to turn to spiritualism for comfort, and no-one would wish to rob anyone of any consolation they may find. It is my conviction, however, that the true Christian believer, who is, as I have tried to show, more rational than the rationalists, is also more spiritual than the spiritualists. It is no part of our business as Christian preachers to ridicule or scorn those who hold other convictions, however mistakenly, but it is our responsibility to proclaim the Gospel in all its richness so that men may not be satisfied with anything less. And what the spiritualists offer seems to me to be so very much less. If I understand them aright, their concern is to prove the fact of survival. But that is not the same thing as the Christian doctrine of immortality. Most spiritualists do in fact believe in the existence of God, but I see no reason why they must do so, any more than people who believe in the 'here and now' need believe in God in consequence. Belief in survival, though interesting, is not of itself a religious belief at all. Personally, I haven't examined the evidence of the spiritualists with enough care to enable me to pronounce for certain on its validity. As far as I have come into touch with it, it seems altogether unconvincing, often grotesquely so, but I'm sure that what our people need in this matter is to be shown how belief in mere survival falls short of the Christian belief in immortality. Any belief which puts survival first, and estimates that prospect independently of God's character and purpose, is a poor substitute for Christian truth, which is concerned not so much with the fact of life hereafter as with its quality and man's glorious destiny as a child of God. 'He which raised up the Lord Jesus, shall raise us up also with Jesus.'

15

The Communion of Saints

OUR consideration in the last chapter of 'The Christian hope of Immortality' leads us naturally to the doctrine of 'The Communion of Saints', which has its place in the Apostles' creed.

Let us consider first of all the significance of the doctrine itself and then its bearing on the content of our preaching. That it has a most important bearing is beyond question. On occasions during a settled ministry in a church, I have invited members of the congregation to submit questions with which they would like me to deal in sermons, and more than once I have been asked: 'What do Christians mean by "the Communion of Saints"?' and I have had similar experiences at Question-time in the open air.

When a man or woman joins the Christian Church, he becomes a member of a visible community whose members worship God together and have fellowship with one another in a particular place. This intimate association, however, is only a part, though doubtless to him the most vital part of the new relationship into which he has entered. Whether he fully realizes it or not, he has come into a new relationship to every other Christian disciple everywhere. He has joined the one society which spans oceans and continents, embraces men of every tribe, tongue and colour and knows no barrier of any kind whatever between man and man. He is a member of the Holy Catholic Church of Jesus Christ. The word 'Catholic' means 'universal' or 'for everybody'. It is because of our common relationship to Jesus as Saviour and Lord that we find ourselves in this new relationship to one another. This is not by a separate act of our own volition but is an inescapable consequence of our response to God in Jesus Christ. The cords of His love which bind us each to

Him bind us also to each other. If the most real things are the spiritual things, we are closer to our fellow Christians of other countries and races than to those of our neighbours with whose aims and ideals we have little in common.

But even that is not the whole of it. The Church is universal not only in extent but in depth. It spans not only oceans and continents, but empires, and we are one not only with our fellow Christians on earth, but with those who now worship the same Lord in heaven. That is what is meant when the Church is described as 'militant on earth, triumphant in heaven'. We are all familiar with the New Testament metaphor of the Christian life as a pilgrimage. We are running a race, finishing a course. Round the ropes that mark off the track is the 'cloud of witnesses', who have already run the race and finished the course. The visible community of Christians round about us is just a small fraction of the redeemed society in the making. We cannot limit our thought of the Church within the narrow frontiers of this world's life. Those who have gone before us in the faith have gone to another world but not to another church.

How deeply this Christian doctrine is embedded in our tradition is amply illustrated by Charles Wesley's hymns.

> . . . all the servants of the King
> In earth and heaven are one.

Indeed, the whole of this hymn ('Come, let us join our friends above') is one of the most lucid and compelling statements of this faith

> One family we dwell in Him
> One Church above, beneath
> Though now divided by the stream
> The narrow stream of death.
> One army of the living God
> At His command we bow;
> Part of His host have crossed the flood
> And part are crossing now.

The reality of this is brought home to us at every Communion service when ' with angels and archangels and all the company of heaven' we glorify God's holy name.

It remains only to suggest some of the implications of this vital Christian truth for our preaching. Consider, for example, what light is thrown on the constant tension between the individual and social aspect of religion, and therefore on the meaning of life itself. 'The New Testament,' John Wesley declared, 'knows nothing of a solitary religion.' And again 'There is no holiness, except social holiness'. We are always individuals, but never merely individual. From the beginning we grow up in a social context. We are nurtured by parents, taught and disciplined at home and in school, and we take our place as adult citizens of a community. Even Robinson Crusoe was not born on his desert island, nor did he remain on it in permanent isolation. As Christians we have our place here and now within the family of God. The fellowship of that family transcends the limitations of time and our destiny will only be realized in eternity as we participate in the joys of the redeemed. This does not imply that our personalities will be merged in a vague ocean of spirit, but rather that they will be enriched and fulfilled in the heavenly community.

It is significant that in the famous eleventh chapter of Hebrews, the heroes of days gone by, Gideon, Samson, Barak and the rest take their place in the catalogue which leads on to the Christian saints of later days, 'God having provided some better thing concerning us that they without us should not be made perfect'. It is surely not fanciful to see a hint here that, in the timeless order of God's eternal world, undeveloped souls may draw on the treasury of life of succeeding generations and fulfil their destiny in the wider community and the unrestricted fellowship of God's other world.

How all this sharpens the issue for this life on earth! What light it sheds on the fellowship of suffering! This life here takes on a new and splendid meaning as we discover ourselves linked through the communion of saints with a purpose, the consummation of which will be more glorious than we can imagine when the family of God is complete and He, Creator, Redeemer, Perfecter, is all in all.

16

The Unchanging Christ

EARLIER in these pages we looked at the message of Advent and sought to relate it to the world we live in today. We noticed the significance of the fact that before we meet together in spirit around the cradle at Bethlehem to worship our newborn King, we are bidden to look forward to His future reign in power and glory.

As we draw to a conclusion I would commend to you as an appropriate theme to be handled on some suitable occasion ' The Unchanging Christ '. Hard upon the heels of Christmas comes the New Year, an event which has no place in the calendar of the Church, but which none the less forces itself on our attention. We cannot for long forget the ceaseless march of time which affects us all and must influence profoundly our outlook on life. This reminder which the New Year brings so soon after we celebrate our Lord's incarnation affords us an opportunity of arresting the attention of our hearers by speaking to the mood in which many of them will find themselves at that season.

It would be difficult to find a better jumping-off point than the well-known description of our Lord as ' The same, yesterday, today and for ever ' (Hebrews 13⁸). We do not know who was the author of the Epistle to the Hebrews, but we know that he belonged to the second generation of Christians and wrote to the Christians of that generation. For him and his readers, Jesus belonged to the world's yesterday.

What he claims is that Jesus was the same to him and those whom he addressed as He had been to the apostles and those who first believed. Not content with that, he waxes bolder and affirms that not only they, but Christians of all succeeding generations would find Jesus to be in their experience precisely what the Christians of New Testament days had found Him to be. The letter was written to Jews who found themselves in a strange new world where this new faith separated them from the world in which they had been born. Moreover they were facing an impending crisis. the full significance of which they were unable to understand. Their grasp of all their new religion had given them was as yet imperfect and the one thing which could brace them for the bitter conflict in which they were engaged and so hard beset was that the Unchanging Christ was with them.

Our situation today has much in common with theirs. Indeed, our world is changing before our very eyes much more rapidly than theirs. More change has taken place in our lifetime in the externals of living, in the outward form and fashion of life and in the world of thought than in all the previous centuries of the Christian era. Someone has remarked that the world of George III was nearer to that of Nebuchadnezzar than to that of George VI. Nor is this process likely to end. We can safely assume that the next century will witness even greater changes than the last and he would be a bold man indeed to prophesy the shape of things a hundred years hence.

It is against such a background that we must needs examine the Christian claim of 'The Unchanging Christ' and at first sight it sounds hardly feasible. How can we maintain that the son of a Galilean carpenter, nineteen hundred years ago, who lived only for about thirty years during which He never travelled outside His own country, can have anything to say to us? Still more, how can we claim that He is 'the Way, the Truth and the Life' for all men?

Let me suggest three answers to that question. Others will

occur as these three are pondered, reinforcing our faith in His changelessness.

First of all, His teaching has stood the test of time. Without attempting to set forth a code of behaviour, which would inevitably have become obsolete as the outward circumstances of life were transformed, our Lord has left us coherent teaching about God, about man, and about the world, which is as relevant today as ever it was. There is no problem facing this new world on which He has not some final word to say. On the contrary, truths which He spiritually perceived, such as the brotherhood of all the human race, have been borne out as history has unfolded itself. The only serious criticism which is levelled at His teaching is that it is too good, and therefore impracticable in this workaday world. Could there be a more convincing tribute?

Secondly, His character remains unchallenged as the pattern for humanity. In Him precept and practice coincided. Others could say 'Love one another'. Only He can add 'as I have loved you'. The cross was erected on Calvary about A.D. 27, but it 'towers o'er all the wrecks of time'. He challenges us not only by what He taught but by what He did and most of all by who He was.

On both these counts it may be urged that it all happened a long time ago. Glorious teaching and glorious living but ever receding glory. But His changelessness chiefly resides in His power to transform human lives. In this He meets man's changeless needs. Lapse of time and distance of space are alike powerless to affect this. When men and women hear the story of our Lord's redemptive love and allow their hearts and minds to go out to Him in glad and free response, their sins are forgiven, they receive power to conquer sin in themselves and they enter into life eternal.

This is because in Jesus was revealed once and for all the character and purpose of the eternal God. 'O Come, let us adore Him, Christ the Lord'.

17

Summing up

WE have considered our need as preachers for a sound grasp of theology as a foundation for our proclamation of the Gospel and, beginning with the Doctrine of God, we have looked in turn at many, if not most, of the great truths which underlie the Gospel. Always our aim has been to suggest how a particular doctrine may be effectively stated in relation to the need of our hearers and the situation in which they live their lives. In the last chapter our theme was 'The Unchanging Christ' and it would indeed be difficult to choose one more appropriate with which to bring these studies to a close. I propose, therefore, to do no more than add a kind of footnote to remind you how, in the unchanging Christ, Christians find the clue to the interpretation of all history. In the New Testament this is the dominant theme of Paul's later Epistles, especially those to the Ephesians and the Colossians. Readers who can give the time to a closer study will find an impressive treatment of it in Dr. John Baillie's *Our Knowledge of God,* especially pages 180-189.

All primitive peoples thought of history as a straight line in which event succeeded event in no significant pattern. The idea of a purpose being worked out through history was entirely absent. Then came the ancient Greek and Roman civilizations with their Indian and Chinese counterparts when the cyclical theory held sway. A notable example of this is to be found in the opening chapter of Ecclesiastes : 'The sun also ariseth and the sun goeth down, and hasteth to his place where he ariseth. . . . That which hath been is that which shall be; and that which hath been done is that which shall be done : and there is no new thing under the sun.'

Curiously enough this conception, utterly alien to Christianity, has found its way into one of our best known Christmas hymns!

> But lo! the days are hastening on
> By prophet bards foretold
> When with the ever circling years
> Comes round the age of gold.

For the Jews history was a drama. It did reveal an unfolding purpose. God was all powerful. Human history was like a line which was descending lower and lower. Things were getting steadily worse and would continue so until the day when God would intervene catastrophically. All sorts of signs and portents would herald this divine intervention when God would scatter His enemies and take the power. In an earlier article we saw how this imagery lay behind the form in which the earliest Christians, cradled in Judaism, entertained the expectation of the second coming of our Lord.

Centuries later came the idea of progress, a surprisingly modern conception undreamed of in the ancient world. According to this theory things were getting better and better. This view was complacently held during the early scientific triumphs of the nineteenth century, but it has been decisively shattered by the events of the last fifty years.

In contrast to these, what is the Christian view? For us Christians, history has a centre and we unconsciously recognize this every time we date a letter. Everything for the Christian is either B.C. or A.D. History patterns itself around those events when the eternal God, who was and is and ever shall be, entered human life with an act of self-disclosure in which His eternal character and purpose were once for all made plain. All that went before can only be understood as leading up to Christ. All that has happened since takes on meaning as it is related to that unique revelation. The eternal Christ is the centre round whom all history ranges itself. He is the centre that determines the beginning and the end for He reveals the principle at the heart of the universe which gives its meaning.

But look back over the long path mankind has travelled. The glimpses of truth vouchsafed to men have been pointers to Him who is the Truth; as we look forward and try to pierce the veil that conceals the future alike in time and in eternity, only He can afford us a firm foundation of hope. The future, we believe, is His as the past has been His, and all things will be summed up in Him; as we look inward and interpret the deepest longings and aspirations of our own hearts, it is in Him and Him alone that we find true peace, the peace of God which passeth all understanding.

> *Yea through life, death, through sorrow and through sinning,*
> *He shall suffice me, for He hath sufficed.*
> *Christ is the End, for Christ is the Beginning,*
> *Christ the Beginning, for the End is Christ.*